Desserts and Ice Creams

A selection of British favourites

Diana Baker

Copyright © 2014 - 2016 Diana Baker

Copyright © 2014 - 2016 Editorial Imagen.
Córdoba, Argentina

Editorialimagen.com
All rights reserved.

Corrected and Revised Edition, July 2016

All rights reserved. No part of this book may be reproduced by any means (including electronic, mechanical or otherwise, such as photocopying, recording or any storage or reproduction of information) without written permission of the author, except for brief portions quoted for review purposes.

All images in this book (cover and interior pictures) are used with permission of: Starsammy, Ewan-M, Whatkatiesbaking.com, Evin DC, NourishingCook, Stu Spivack, Janet Hudson, Sistak, Larry Page, Kelly Reeves, Amazing Almonds, Kristina (Meringue Bake Shop), Phil Denton, Wonderyort, Mark Pasc, The Pudding Club, James E. Petts, Lori L. Stalteri, Feli, Theory of Sherry E., Aonghus Flynn, Mydogivana, E. Skene, Srgpicker, Fugzu, Girl Interrupted Eating, Javier Delgado, Jem, Sharkey, Hfb, Ward van Wanrooij, Daa Nell, Avlxyz.

CATEGORY: Recipes

Printed in the United States of America

ISBN-13:
ISBN-10:

Content

Introduction 1

Hints to Ensure Success 3

To Prove the Temperature of the Oven 5

Weights and Measures 7

Recipes for Desserts 9

    To Cook Dried Fruit so that it Tastes Fresh 11
    Almond Baked Apples 12
    Apples a L'Escoffier 14
    Apricot Snow 15
    Fritters 16
    Apple Fritters 18
    Baked Cake Pudding 19
    Bombshells 20
    Chocolate and Banana Pudding 21
    Chocolate Mousse 23
    Chocolate Mousse – II 24
    Rich Chocolate Trifle 25
    College Pudding 26
    Cottage Pudding 27
    Orange Cream 28
    Norwegian Sherry Cream 29
    Cumberland Pudding 30
    Custard 31
    Baked Honey Custard 32

Venus Custard 33
Snowflakes 34
Fairy Pudding 36
Strawberry Fluff 37
French Fruit Pudding 38
Heavenly Pie 39
Lemon Pudding 40
Hot or Cold Lemon Pudding 41
Fruit Meringues 42
Puffy Jam Omelette 43
Pain Perdue 45
Shrove Tuesday Pancake 46
Royal Pancakes 47
Peach Pie 49
Stewed Pineapple 50
Plumbers Revenge 51
Prune Whip 53
Raspberry Pudding 54
Rice Pudding 55
Strawberry Mousse 56
Tipsy Squire 57
Devonshire Trifle 58
Yam Pudding 60

Boiled Puddings 61

Key Recipe for Suet Paste for Puddings 63
Apple Pudding I 64
Apple Pudding II 65
Aunt Amy's Pudding 66
Chocolate Pudding 67
Cup Pudding 68
Six Cup Pudding 69
Grandma's Christmas Pudding 70

A Good Homemade Christmas Pudding 72
Dundee Pudding 75
Essex Pudding 77
Fig Pudding 78
Jam and Marmalade Pudding 80
Jemima's Pudding 82
Steamed Macaroon Pudding 83
Melbourne Pudding 84
Mincemeat Roly Poly 85
Novelty Pudding 87
Orange Pudding with Sauce 88
Peach Pudding 89
Plain Suet Pudding 91
Plum Pudding (Spotted Dick) 92
Spiff Pudding 94
Sponge Pudding 95

Sweet Sauces 97

Brandy Sauce 99
Brown Sugar Sauce 100
Caramel Sauce 101
Caramel Mocha Sauce 102
Fruit Sauce 103
Hot Chocolate Sauce 104
Vanilla Custard Sauce 105
Diplomatic Sauce 106
Rummage Fruit Cream Sauce 107
White Wine Sauce 108

Desserts with Gelatine 109

Gelatine 111

Babaroise 112
American Custard 113
Apricot Custard Sponge 115
Sherry Fluff 117
Fruit and White Wine Jelly 118
Lemon Jelly 120
Orange and Egg Jelly 121
Plum Jelly 122
Milk Gelatine 123
Sunset Mousse 124
Lemon Snow 125
Snow Pudding 126
Cold Chocolate Soufflé 127
Spanish Cream 128

Fruit Pies and Tarts 129

Pastry 131
Never-Fail Pie Crust for Beginners 132
Family Short Pastry 133
Rough Puff Pastry 134
An Easy Piecrust to Try 135
Scotch Apple Pie 136
Tasty Apple Roll 137
Special Fruit Tart 138
Bakewell Tart 140
Caramel Tart 141
Citron Pudding or Tart 142
Coconut Pie 144
Grape Tart 145
Easy Grape Tart 146
Middle West Lemon Pie 147
Mock Mince Pies 149
Orange Tart 150

    Orange Tartlets 151

    Raisin Nut Tart 152

    Rhubarb Tart 153

Ice Cream 155

    Carioca Ice Cream 157

    Burnt Ice Cream 158

    Easy Ice Cream 159

    Lemon Cream 160

    Mocha Ice Cream 161

    Fruity Ice Cream 162

    Raspberry Ice Cream 163

    Russian Ice Cream 164

    Strawberry Ice Cream 165

    Vanilla Ice Cream 166

    Chocolate Ice Cream I 167

    Never-Fail Vanilla Ice Cream 168

Variations of Never-Fail Ice Cream 169

    Coffee Ice Cream 171

    Orange Ice Cream 172

    Tutti Frutti Ice Cream 173

    Chocolate Ice Cream II 174

    Fresh Strawberry Ice Cream 175

    Fresh Peach Ice Cream 176

More Books of Interest 177

Spanish Related Books 181

Introduction

It is so good to finish a delicious meal with an even more delicious dessert! In fact, the dessert is the best part! And for most English people something sweet is something to look forward to, any time of the day. It probably has something to do with the climate where a hot pudding is almost a must.

In this recipe book you will find more than 130 British favourites for desserts which include also: Boiled Puddings, Tarts, Fruit Tarts, Desserts with Gelatine, Sauces to accompany the desserts, and Ice Cream, which are popular the world over.

You'll find the recipes are not at all difficult and they are easy to follow and also using everyday ingredients.

I'm sure you will find many to your taste and I hope they even become popular with the whole family and get to be long time favourites too.

Hints to Ensure Success

- Always read the recipe through carefully and understand it before starting. Then collect together and prepare all the ingredients to be used.

- Always sift the flour.

- Always stir in the same direction.

- Grease all cake tins except when making angel and sponge cakes.

- Never bang the oven door.

- Always work neatly; use as few utensils as possible, and clear up as the cooking proceeds.

- Never mix new flour with old.

- Never begrudge the time you spend on good mixing.

Cakes are often spoiled by over beating after the baking powder has been added; it is therefore advisable to add the baking powder, sifted with a small quantity of the flour, last.

One's usual experience is that if you take no care and make a hurried cake for the family, it is lighter than the cake made for the special occasion. The reason is probably because too much beating has been done after baking powder has been added, or that too much flour has been used.

To Prove the Temperature of the Oven

A simple and effective method of proving the heat of the oven when no thermometer is available:

Heat the oven for 10 minutes, then, put a piece of white paper in the centre of the oven. The temperature of the oven will be correct if the paper becomes brown in the time specified below:

Oven	Degrees	Paper
Very hot	446ºF–500ºF	½ minute
Hot	392ºF-428ºF	1 minute
Moderate	338ºF-374ºF	1 ½ minutes
Slow	320ºF	2 minutes

Electric and Gas equivalents

275°F = 140°C or Gas Mark 1
300°F = 150°C or Gas Mark 2
325°F = 165°C or Gas Mark 3
350°F = 180°C or Gas Mark 4
375°F = 190°C or Gas Mark 5
400°F = 200°C or Gas Mark 6
425°F = 220°C or Gas Mark 7
450°F = 230°C or Gas Mark 8

Weights and Measures

All containers used for measuring should be filled level, unless otherwise stated in the recipe, smoothing off any surplus with a knife.

When a cup is indicated, a cup holding ½ pint should be used.

1 Teaspoon equals 5 g or 60 drops

1 Dessertspoon equals 10 g or 2 teaspoons

1 Tablespoon equals 15 g or 3 teaspoons

1 wine glass equals 100 g or 4 tablespoons

1 cup equals ½ pint or ¼ litre or 16 tablespoons

1 lb. equals 16 ounces or 460 g

½ lb. equals 8 ounces or 230 g

1 ounce equals 28 ½ g

3 ½ cups flours are equivalent to .... 480 g or 1 lb.

2 cups oatmeal flour.................................. 480 g or 1 lb

2 cups granulated sugar .... 400 g or 14 ozs

2 ½ cups icing sugar................................. 300 g or 11 ozs

2 1/4 cups brown sugar............................ 500 g or l lb.

1 cup seedless raisins .... 200 g or 7 ozs

1 cup currants etc. .... 200 g or 7 ozs

2 cups chopped nuts .... 240 g or ½ lb.

1 cup butter or lard .... 230 g or ½ lb.

Recipes for Desserts

To Cook Dried Fruit so that it Tastes Fresh

1 cup sugar
4 or 5 cups water
2 or 3 cups dried fruit
Juice of 1 lemon

Mix the sugar and water in a fair sized saucepan and boil till sugar is dissolved.

Put the dried fruit into a basin of cold water then pare and drop each piece into the boiling syrup.

Cover the pan with lid and boil for 5 minutes or until the fruit is tender but not broken.

Take the lid off and allow to boil for a few minutes until the syrup thickens a little.

Let it cool in the saucepan.

Note:

The juice of a lemon improves the taste.

Almond Baked Apples

2 tablespoons butter
4 tablespoons sugar
1 egg
3 tablespoons breadcrumbs
4 tablespoons almonds
4 large apples
A few chopped dates

Blanche and chop the almonds and mix with the chopped dates and half the sugar.

Beat the egg and the rest of the sugar together. Stir in two thirds of the breadcrumbs.

Peel and core the apples without breaking them. Coat the apples with a little flour. Melt the butter in a fireproof dish in the oven.

Fill the centres of the apples with the almonds, sugar and dates, and pour the mixture of the breadcrumbs, egg and sugar over the apples.

Sprinkle remaining third part of the breadcrumbs on top and bake in a moderate oven until tender and brown.

Tip:

When you bake apples, try using sultanas instead of sugar.

Core the apples and stuff them with washed sultanas. Slit the skin round with a sharp knife to prevent them from bursting.

Diana Baker

Apples a L'Escoffier

Some cooking apples
A little lemon juice
A few tablespoons of vanilla essence
Powdered sugar
Butter
A little brandy

Core some cooking apples.

Peel them and parboil them for 2 minutes in boiling water, containing a little lemon juice.

Then set them in a buttered saucepan.

Add a few tablespoons of vanilla flavoured syrup. Cover and cook in the oven.

Dish them out on little circles of sponge cake.

Cream the butter with an equal weight of powdered sugar and a little brandy.

Then fill the centre of each apple with this creamy mixture.

Cover the apples with their own syrup, slightly thickened with apricot pureé.

Apricot Snow

1 tin of apricots
2 egg whites
Sugar to taste
1 teaspoon lemon juice

Drain the fruit and rub through a sieve or heat with a fork.

Add a little lemon juice and sugar.

Beat the whites to a stiff froth and add the apricot pureé very gently.

Chill and serve in glasses with whipped cream.

Fritters

This recipe makes a very good batter

2 tablespoons flour
½ tablespoon butter
½ tablespoon salt
2 eggs or 1 egg and 1 teaspoon baking powder
Milk
Sugar
Lemon juice
Hot lard for frying

Divide the whites from the yolks and beat them separately.

Beat the butter to a cream,

Put the flour into a bowl, stir in the creamed butter.

Add the salt and moisten with sufficient warm milk to make it of a proper consistency – a batter that will drop form the spoon.

Rub down any lumps and stir well. Add the yolks and lastly the well whisked whites.

Tips:

- The batter is better if mixed some hours before the fritters are made.

- Almost any kind of fruit will make fritters. The fruit

must be peeled, cored or stoned and cut in rings.

- Apple, apricot, peach, orange, pineapple and banana make delicious fritters.

- Before frying the fruit, coat with powdered sugar before dipping into the batter.

Apple Fritters

Apples
2 tablespoons flour
1 egg
A pinch of salt
½ glass white wine or beer
1 teaspoon cinnamon
Oil for frying
A little hot water

Beat the egg with the flour. Add the salt and stir well with a little hot water, the wine (or beer) and the cinnamon.

Beat well and leave for one hour.

Cut the apples into rings, core and dip them in the batter and fry in boiling oil.

Baked Cake Pudding

2 tablespoons butter
2 tablespoons sugar
1 small cup flour
1 egg
A pinch of salt
1 teaspoon baking powder
A handful of currants
A little milk

Beat the butter and sugar well together.

Add the flour, egg, salt, baking powder, milk and currants.

Make the batter thinner than for a cake.

Butter a dish and bake in hot oven for 30 minutes.

Diana Baker

Bombshells

1 tin or peaches
A little butter, sugar and cinnamon
A little brandy

Drain the tin of peaches.

Place the peaches on a baking dish.

Fill each cavity with a little butter, sugar and cinnamon.

Bake for 20 minutes in a moderate oven (350°F).

Transfer them to a serving dish.

Sprinkle with sugar.

Pour some warmed brandy over them and send flaming to the table.

Chocolate and Banana Pudding

The recipe is sufficient for 6 people.

¾ cup flour
3 bananas
1½ heaped tablespoons cocoa
1 egg
3 tablespoons butter
½ cup sugar
1 teaspoon baking powder
Milk

Rub the butter into the flour.

Add the sugar, cocoa and baking powder and mix together.

Peel and slice the bananas and mix with the dry ingredients.

Beat up the egg and add with the amount of milk required. Mix all together.

Put into a small greased pie dish.

Bake in a moderately hot oven for 45 minutes.

Turn out on to a hot dish and serve with hot custard.

Vanilla custard:

2 egg yolks

2 tablespoons sugar
1 cup sugar
1 teaspoon vanilla essence

Beat the yolks and add sugar gradually.

Boil the milk and pour over the beaten egg yolks, beating all the time.

Thicken in double saucepan, stirring constantly.

Flavour with vanilla.

Chocolate Mousse

Using these proportions you can make the quantity desired. 3 eggs make about 7 glasses.

1 egg
1 teaspoon castor sugar
1 bar chocolate

Break up chocolate and soften in a bowl over boiling water.

Separate yolks and whites of eggs. Beat up yolks and add the chocolate.

Mix well and press out all the lumps.

Whip up the whites stiffly and fold them into the chocolate mixture.

Lastly, add the sugar.

Then beat all together well.

Put the mixture into small glasses and leave for 3 hours in refrigerator to set.

Cover each with whipped cream and decorate them with hard chocolate or chopped walnuts.

Chocolate Mousse – II

Allow for each person:

1 tablespoon chocolate powder
1 tablespoon cream
1 egg white
Sugar to taste

Beat the egg white well and the cream separately.

Beat both to a stiff froth and then fold them into each other.

Add the grated chocolate little by little, folding it in lightly so that it is well mixed without the mousse losing its lightness.

Sweeten to taste with castor sugar.

Cool in refrigerator before serving.

Rich Chocolate Trifle

1 pint of milk
2 eggs
Sugar to taste
2 bars of ground chocolate
A small piece of butter

Prepare a chocolate custard with the above ingredients.

2 packets sponge fingers
1 cup chopped nuts

Place in a pyrex dish a covering of chocolate custard and a few nuts, then some sponge fingers.

Repeat this procedure placing the sponge fingers crosswise on each layer. Use up all the sponge fingers.

Place in the refrigerator until set then turn out of dish onto a plate and cover with whipped cream.

Decorate with grated chocolate and nuts. This must be made the day before serving.

College Pudding

1 cup flour
1 teaspoon baking powder
1 tablespoon butter
1½ cups sugar
1 cup milk
1 egg
A pinch of salt

Beat the butter and sugar to a cream.

Add the eggs beaten with the milk.

Then the flour and baking powder sifted together and beat well.

Bake 2 hours in a moderate oven.

Cottage Pudding

1/3 cup butter
¾ cup sugar
1½ cups flour
1 egg
2 teaspoons baking powder
1 teaspoon vanilla
½ teaspoon salt
½ cup milk

Cream the butter and add the sugar gradually.

Then add the egg. Beat well.

Sift flour with baking powder and salt and then add to the butter mixture, alternating with the milk.

Add the vanilla.

Line a shallow pan with greased paper.

Pour in the cake batter and bake for about 35 minutes.

Spread with jam and serve with a jug of cream.

Diana Baker

Orange Cream

Juice of 6 oranges
6 eggs
1 cup cream
½ cup sugar

Strain the juice of the oranges.

Beat the eggs and mix with the cream.

Stir in the juice and the sugar.

Put into a double boiler and cook till it thickens.

Serve cold,

Norwegian Sherry Cream

This quantity is sufficient for three portions.

3 tablespoons sugar
3 eggs
½ cream
2 cocktail glasses of sherry

Stir the egg yolks, the sugar and sherry over a slow fire until it thickens, but it must not boil.

Then set aside to cool.

When quite cool add the cream which has been beaten stiff.

Lastly add the stiffly beaten whites of eggs.

Serve in custard cups, well chilled.

Cumberland Pudding

2 tablespoons butter
4½ tablespoons sugar
2 eggs
½ cup flour
2 cups milk
½ cup sherry
1 large lemon

Melt the butter.

Add the flour then add the milk gradually and stir until it boils.

Remove from fire and add the grated lemon rind and juice.

Then add the eggs one by one. Stir in quickly.

Add the sugar and lastly the sherry.

Pour into a buttered soufflé dish and bake for about 30 minutes in a moderate oven.

Custard

3 cups milk
5 eggs and 2 yolks
¾ cups sugar
1 teaspoon vanilla essence
A pinch of salt

Beat the eggs lightly with the sugar.

Add the milk and vanilla.

Melt a little of the sugar in a saucepan and when brown spread into a pudding basin.

Then pour in the egg and milk preparation.

Place basin in a saucepan of boiling water until the custard sets.

The custard can also be cooked in the oven if placed in a dish of water.

Turn out and serve either hot or cold.

Baked Honey Custard

3 eggs slightly beaten
3 cups milk
A pinch of salt
¼ cup honey
½ teaspoon vanilla essence (optional)

Melt the honey until it runs, then stir in the eggs.

Stir in the milk, salt and vanilla essence.

Divide between 6 buttered, medium sized, custard cups.

Place them in a pan containing a little warm water.

Bake in a moderate oven until firm and brown, about 30 minutes, or bake in a large dish for about 45 minutes but stand the dish in a pan of warm water as for the individual custards.

Serve with cream or with 1 tablespoon jam boiled up with sufficient water to make a liquid sauce.

Venus Custard

12 yolks
6 whites of eggs
Sugar to taste
1 pint of cream (2 cups)
1 oz gelatine
A little milk
Candied peel
Glacé fruit
A glass of brandy or liqueur

Take a quart mould, butter it well and place candied peel and pieces of glacé fruit around the mould.

Make a custard with the eggs and sugar.

Add the cream and mix lightly together.

Pour it into the mould.

Dissolve the gelatine in sufficient milk to fill the mould up to the top.

When nearly cold stir in a glass of brandy or liqueur.

Serve cold with cream.

Snowflakes

6 yolks
6 egg whites
Sugar to taste
A little more than a pint of fresh milk
A little vanilla essence or other flavouring

Separate the yolks from the whites.

Beat the whites to a stiff froth with a little finely powdered sugar.

Have ready a full pint of fresh milk, well sweetened and flavoured with vanilla or other essence.

When it boils, drop in, one by one, tablespoons full of the frothed whites and when set remove each with a slicer.

Arrange the patches of snowflakes on a large dish. By varying the quantity dropped in (some small patches and some larger patches) you will obtain a prettier arrangement. The large patches look better in the centre.

When the milk has boiled a little, mix with it the beaten egg yolks slowly and very gradually until all is used and it has become thick.

Pour this mixture amongst and around the snow but not over them. Serve cold.

Fairy Pudding

2 tablespoons cornflour (cornstarch)
2 tablespoons sugar
1½ cups water
1 lemon
2 egg whites

Mix the cornflour with some water.

Boil the rest of the water with the lemon peel and sugar for 2 minutes.

Add the cornflour and juice of the lemons.

Boil for 2 minutes.

Cool and then add the beaten whites.

Cool until ready to serve.

Serve with a custard made with the yolks.

Strawberry Fluff

This recipe is sufficient for 2 portions.

2 egg whites
2 tablespoons strawberry jam

Beat the whites to a stiff froth.

Fold in the jam.

Put into a mould, previously wetted with cold water and steam for about 10 minutes or until firm.

When nearly cold turn out.

Make a thin custard with the 2 yolks and pour around the dish.

Diana Baker

French Fruit Pudding

Bread
Milk
Fruit
A little sugar
3 or 4 eggs

Soak some slices of bread in milk (brioche or milk bread) then fill a dish with alternate layers of bread and summer fruit such as cherries, apricots etc. and a little sugar.

Then pour on to this, 3 or 4 well beaten eggs and bake slowly.

Can be eaten hot or cold, or can be turned out as a jelly.

Heavenly Pie

The recipe is sufficient for 6 to 8 portions.
1½ cups sugar
¼ teaspoon cream of tartar
4 eggs
3 tablespoons lemon juice
1 tablespoon lemon rind, finely grated
1½ cups cream

Sift 1 cup of the sugar and the cream of tartar.

Beat the whites until stiff but not dry.

Then gradually add the sugar mixture, continuing to beat until thoroughly blended.

Use to line the bottom and sides of a 9" or 10" greased pie plate, being careful not to spread too close to rim.

Bake in slow oven for 1 hour then cool. Beat the egg yolks slightly.

Then stir in remaining ½ cup of sugar and the lemon juice and rind.

Cook in top of double boiler until very thick, for about 10 minutes.

Remove and cool.

Whip the cream, combine half of it with the lemon egg mixture, and use to fill shell.

Cover with the remaining whipped cream.

Chill in refrigerator about 24 hours.

Lemon Pudding

3 heaped tablespoons sugar
1 lemon
3 heaped tablespoons flour
2 eggs
2 cups milk
2 tablespoons butter

Whisk the eggs and sugar together until thick and creamy.

Grate the lemon rind finely and stir in with the flour.

Warm the butter just sufficiently to melt it and add.

Stir in the milk gradually and mix all together.

Turn the mixture into a well greased pie dish.

Bake in a moderate oven. It will take about 45 minutes to cook.

Sprinkle with castor sugar and serve in the same dish.

Hot or Cold Lemon Pudding

The recipe is sufficient for 6 portions.

2 cups water
1 tablespoon cornflour (cornstarch)
1 lemon
2 eggs
16 sponge cakes
1 cup sugar

Mix the cornflour with the water.

Add sugar, grated rind and juice of the lemon and the yolks of the eggs.

Stir over the stove until the mixture thickens, then cook for 5 minutes, still stirring.

Put a layer of this into the pie dish, then a layer of sponge fingers broken up.

Repeat this until all the sponge cakes are used up.

Whisk the whites of the eggs to a stiff froth.

Add a little sugar and pile on the top.

Put in the oven to set for about 10 minutes.

Fruit Meringues

5 large meringue shells
Some stewed red currants and raspberries
½ cup cream
A little sugar
Vanilla
Angelica or pistachio nuts

Turn the cold stewed fruit into a colander and let it drain thoroughly.

Whisk the cream until thick, sweeten and flavour to taste.

Take meringue shells and carefully press in a little of the meringue on the flat side, fill them with fruit and top them with the cream.

Decorate with currants and nuts.

Puffy Jam Omelette

The recipe is sufficient for two portions.

¼ butter
2 dessertspoons sugar
3 eggs
¼ teaspoon vanilla essence
A pinch of salt
Jam

Rub the pan with salt and wipe.

Melt butter in it making sure to moisten sides of pan with it.

Separate the yolks from the whites and beat separately.

Add sugar and essence to the yolks and a pinch of salt to whites.

Mix all together lightly and pour into buttered frying pan.

Shake over low flame till set. Then put into slow oven till pale gold on top.

Slip from pan to warmed dish. Put jam in the middle and fold. Serve at once.

Pain Perdue

Stale bread
Hot milk
A little vanilla essence or rum
Egg yolks
Cinnamon
Butter for frying

Cut slices of stale bread ½ inch thick and soak in hot milk flavoured with vanilla.

When thoroughly soaked, drain and coat with beaten egg yolk.

Fry in butter then dust with sugar and cinnamon.

Serve hot.

Shrove Tuesday Pancake

6 eggs
2 tablespoons flour
½ teaspoon of baking powder
Milk

Beat the eggs to a froth, the yolks and whites together.

Add the flour and baking powder and sufficient milk to make it the consistency of thin cream.

Take a frying pan, warm it and melt a piece of butter about the size of a small walnut.

Then pour in sufficient of the mixture to just cover the surface of the pan.

As soon as it begins to harden, slip a pastry knife under it, shake the pan to loosen the half-cooked pancake, and then with a dexterous turn of the wrist, toss the pancake in the air and catch it in the pan with the uncooked side downward.

Cook it for a minute, fold it four times, squeeze a few drops of lemon juice over it and sprinkle with sifted sugar.

Serve smoking hot with lemon and sugar.

Royal Pancakes

1 cup flour
1 cup milk
2 egg whites
Grated rind of 1 lemon
¼ teaspoon salt
3 egg yolks
½ cup sifted icing sugar
Butter for frying

Beat egg yolks in a bowl. Stir in milk then the flour sifted with salt and sugar.

Add the rind.

Beat egg whites till stiff.

Fold into the mixture. Melt a spoonful of butter in a frying pan.

Add only 1 tablespoon of the batter.

Tip pan from side to side until batter covers the bottom.

Fry till brown below, then turn and brown on the other side. Pile on a hot plate.

When all are ready, dip the pancakes in the sauce.

Roll and serve at once.

Royal Sauce for Pancakes:

¼ cup butter (2 ozs)
¼ teaspoon lemon essence
Grated rind of 1 orange
1 glass of rum or Curaçao
1 cup of icing sugar
¾ teaspoon vanilla essence

Beat the butter to a cream and stir in sugar by degrees.

Add the lemon juice, essence and the rind and juice of the orange.

Melt over boiling water.

Add the rum or Curaçao.

Peach Pie

6 peaches
2 tablespoons butter creamed
½ cup sugar
1 egg
1 cup flour
1 teaspoon baking powder
Milk

Stew gently the peaches then lay them in a dish.

Make a cake mixture – cream the butter and the sugar.

Add the well beaten egg then the flour and the baking powder alternately with a little milk until it is of the consistency of a stiff batter.

Place the cake mixture over the peaches and bake in a moderate oven from 30 to 45 minutes.

Serve with whipped cream.

Stewed Pineapple

1 pineapple
2 cups of water
1 cup of sugar

Peel the pineapple and with a knife scrape the pulp that remains in the interior of the rind.

Put it in a saucepan with the hard part of the centre of the pineapple.

Add the water and sugar.

Make a syrup with these ingredients, allowing it to simmer for 15 minutes.

Then strain and put the syrup again in the saucepan, boiling in it the sliced pineapple, a few at a time, for 2 minutes.

Serve cold with cream.

Plumbers Revenge

10 small sponge cakes
2 cups rich custard
4 egg yolks, hard boiled
½ cup butter
½ cup castor sugar
¼ cup ground almonds
Grated rind of 1 small lemon
A few drops of vanilla essence
1 glass of sherry

For the custard:

2 cups fresh milk
4 eggs
¾ cup castor sugar

Make the custard in the usual way.

Remove from fire and when cold add the essence of vanilla and sherry, stirring with a wooden spoon.

Cut each sponge cake into four.

Arrange them in a glass dish and pour over the custard when cold. Set aside for 2 hours.

Boil the eggs quite hard.

When cold, remove the yolks.

Put them in a bowl and work smooth with a wooden spoon.

Then add the creamed butter, castor sugar, ground almonds and grated lemon rind.

Work well and quickly together, as the appearance of the dessert depends on this.

Lastly, press the mixture through a colander on to the top of the custard. It will fall like curds.

Decorate with glacé cherries and angelica.

Prune Whip

2/3 cup stewed prunes
5 egg whites
½ cup sugar
½ tablespoon lemon juice

Rub the prunes through a strainer. Add sugar and cook 5 minutes.

The mixture should be of the consistency of marmalade.

Beat egg whites until stiff.

Add prune mixture gradually when cold.

Pile lightly on buttered pudding dish.

Bake for 30 minutes in slow oven. Serve cold with custard.

Custard:

2 egg yolks
2 tablespoons sugar
1 cup milk
1 teaspoon vanilla essence

Beat the yolks and add the sugar gradually.

Boil the milk and pour over the beaten egg yolks all the time.

Thicken in double saucepan, stirring constantly.

Raspberry Pudding

2 tablespoons cornflour (cornstarch)
1 small tin of raspberries
1 cup sugar
2 cups water

Mix the sugar, cornflour and pinch of salt together and slowly stir in the water.

Cook until the cornflour is done.

Add the juice and fruit and chill.

Serve in a glass dish garnish with whipped cream.

Rice Pudding

2 large cups of milk
1/3 cup rice
2/3 cup sugar
1/3 cup seedless raisins
1 small stick cinnamon
1/2 teaspoon salt

Wash the rice in several waters, mix with the other ingredients and bring to the boil.

Simmer for 15 minutes then put into a buttered baking dish and continue cooking in the oven at a moderate temperature or if preferred, continue simmering in double saucepan.

Serve either hot or cold, with a jug of cream.

Strawberry Mousse

This recipe is sufficient for 8 portions.

3½ cups fresh cream
3 egg yolks
1 dessertspoon icing sugar
1 cup crushed strawberries
2 or 3 drops of colouring
A little whipped cream and a few strawberries for decoration

Whip the cream till firm.

Add the yolks one by one with the sugar. Mix with a wooden spoon.

When thoroughly mixed, add the crushed strawberries and colouring.

Place the mousse in a fancy mould and freeze. When ready to serve, turn out the mousse onto a plate and decorate with whipped cream and fresh strawberries.

Tipsy Squire

1 small sponge cake
½ cup blanched almonds
1 liqueur glass Benedictine
1 cup sherry
1 cup cream
Sugar to taste

Put the sponge cake into a glass bowl.

Stick the sliced almonds all over it.

Drench with sherry and let stand for 1 hour.

Sweeten the cream to taste and whip to a soft froth.

Flavour with the liqueur and spread over the cake.

Diana Baker

Devonshire Trifle

2 dozen lady fingers
8 macaroons
1/3 cup blanched and cut almonds
¼ cup apple jelly
½ cup Madeira wine
1/3 cup good brandy
1 cup of cream
Vanilla custard

Strew the sponge fingers and macaroons in the bottom of a glass dish, and moisten them with brandy and Madeira.

Drop spoonfuls of jelly over the surface, cover this with custard, sprinkle whipped cream which has been flavoured with a little of the Madeira wine and sweetened.

Whipped cream is used as a substitute for clotted cream.

For the custard:

2 cups fresh milk
4 eggs
¾ cup castor sugar

Make the custard in the usual way.

Remove from fire and when cold add essence of vanilla and sherry, stirring with a wooden spoon.

Yam Pudding

2 cups grated raw yams (sweet potatoes)
¼ cup molasses
½ cup brown sugar
1½ cups milk
1 egg
2 tablespoons melted butter
Grated peel of 1 orange
2 teaspoons lemon juice
1 teaspoon cinnamon
½ teaspoon ginger
½ teaspoon salt

Mix together the grated yams, sugar, molasses, spices, salt and melted butter.

Add beaten egg and milk and pour into a buttered baking dish.

Bake in hot oven for 1 hour.

Serve hot with cream.

Boiled Puddings

Key Recipe for Suet Paste for Puddings

- Suet paste for puddings is made by mixing chopped suet with flour and making the whole into a smooth paste with water.

- The richness of the paste or crust depends upon the quality and quantity of the suet, the rule being, the more suet the richer the crust.

- For making a good suet crust the suet must be chopped very fine and you must avoid lumps.

A good ordinary crust, fairly rich, can be made by mixing

1 lb flour to ½ lb suet and ¼ teaspoon salt.

Mix it with sufficient water to make into a stiff paste.

Flour a board and roll out the paste to the required thickness -a bit less than ¼ inch thick for fruit puddings.

For an ordinary good pudding use:

2 cups flour
1¼ cups suet
1 teaspoon baking powder
A pinch of salt
A little water for mixing

Apple Pudding I

6 apples
2 cups sugar
1 piece of stick vanilla
1 lemon
5 eggs
2 cups milk
3 tablespoons sugar
Sponge fingers or biscuits
Brandy

Peel and core the apples and cook with a very little water. When cooked, pass through a sieve, or mash well with a fork.

Now make a syrup with cups of sugar and the vanilla. When it has thickened a little, add the mashed apples and boil quickly for 10 minutes.

Add the juice of the lemon and leave to cool.

Beat the eggs separately with 3 tablespoons of sugar, the milk and grated lemon rind.

Prepare a mould with burnt sugar.

Place at the bottom and all around the sides the sponge fingers, or pieces of biscuit, soaked in brandy.

Make a layer of the mashed apples then cover with sponge fingers and so on, alternating, until the mould is full.

When quite full, add the beaten egg mixture and steam for 2 hours.

Apple Pudding II

Any fresh fruit, such as plum, blackberry etc. may be substituted for the apple.

Suet paste
4 tablespoons sliced apples
1 teaspoon finely shred suet
6 cloves
1 tablespoon sugar or 1 tablespoon currants

Line a pudding bowl with the suet paste.

Fill it with layers consisting of the sliced apples, the suet, cloves and the sugar.

When full, fold it over, cover with a well-floured cloth or greaseproof paper.

Boil for 2 hours and serve with cream.

Aunt Amy's Pudding

1¾ cups flour
1 cup suet, finely chopped
1 cup treacle
3 tablespoons cream
2 eggs
Rind and juice of 1 lemon
A few strips of candied peel

Mix all the ingredients and beat well.

Put into buttered basin, covered with grease proof paper, and boil from 3½ to 4 hours.

Chocolate Pudding

2 tablespoons butter
2 squares grated chocolate
¾ cup milk
½ cup sugar
1 cup flour
1 teaspoon baking powder
1 egg lightly beaten
A little vanilla essence
A pinch of salt

Cream the butter.

Add the sugar and well beaten egg, flour, baking powder, chocolate, salt and milk.

Mix well, put into a well greased pudding basin and steam for 50 minutes.

Cup Pudding

1 cup chopped suet
1 cup brown sugar
1 cup sultanas
1 cup milk
1 cup currants
1 cup flour
1 cup breadcrumbs
½ teaspoon bicarbonate of soda
2 eggs

Mix the dry ingredients and fruit.

Add the bicarbonate of soda dissolved in a little milk.

Beat in the eggs and add the rest of the milk.

Steam for 3 hours in a well greased mould.

Six Cup Pudding

1 cup flour
1 cup sugar
1 cup breadcrumbs
1 cup jam, sultanas or dried figs
1 egg and fill the cup up with milk
1 cup butter or lard
1 teaspoon baking powder

Mix the flour and butter.

Add the dry ingredients then the jam, egg and milk.

Boil in a buttered basin for 2 hours.

The benefit of this recipe is that the size of the cup can be varied to suit the size of the family.

Diana Baker

Grandma's Christmas Pudding

This recipe makes 1 large pudding

1 lbs suet
1 lbs raisins
1 lbs currants
9 ozs breadcrumbs
2½ tablespoons flour
2½ ozs peel
½ nutmeg
4 eggs
½ lb sugar
A little less than a wine glass of brandy
A little less than a wine glass of sherry
¼ pint of porter (bitter beer)
¼ oz bitter almonds
A little milk

Stone and cut each raisin in half, but do not chop them.

Wash, pick and dry the currants, and mince the suet finely.

Cut the candied peel into thin slices and grate down the bread into fine crumbs.

When all these dry ingredients are prepared, mix them well together with the sugar, then moisten with the eggs, which should be well beaten, and the liquid ingredients.

Stir well so that everything may be very thoroughly blended.

Press the pudding into a buttered mould.

Cover with greased paper and tie down tightly with a floured cloth.

Boil for 8 hours or more, the longer the better.

Boil again before serving for another 5 hours.

When ready to serve, pour a wineglass of rum or brandy over it and set alight.

The pudding should be brought to the table all aflame.

A Good Homemade Christmas Pudding

This recipe is sufficient for 12 to 15 people.

1 lb breadcrumbs
1 lb stoned raisins
1 lb currants
1 lb sultanas
1 lb chopped suet – must be as fine as course flour
½ lb mixed candied peel
1 grated nutmeg
¼ lb flour
½ lb sugar
½ pint sherry
¼ pint rum
2 ozs sweet almonds
2 ozs bitter almonds
1 oz mixed spice
5 eggs
Juice of 2 lemons
2 apples, peeled and chopped

Stone and cut each raisin in half, but do not chop them.

Wash, pick and dry the currants, and mince the suet finely.

Cut the candied peel into thin slices and grate down the bread into fine crumbs.

When all these dry ingredients are prepared, mix them well together with the sugar, then moisten with the eggs, which should be well beaten, and the liquid ingredients.

Stone and cut each raisin in half, but do not chop them.

Wash, pick and dry the currants, and mince the suet finely.

Cut the candied peel into thin slices and grate down the bread into fine crumbs.

When all these dry ingredients are prepared, mix them well together with the sugar, then moisten with the eggs, which should be well beaten, and the liquid ingredients.

Stir well so that everything may be very thoroughly blended.

Press the pudding into a buttered mould.

Cover with greased paper and tie down tightly with a floured cloth.

Boil for 8 hours or more, the longer the better and the

blacker they become.

They should be made several days before Christmas and then given a second boiling of not less than three hours before serving.

When ready to serve, pour a wineglass of rum or brandy over it and set alight.

The pudding should be brought to the table all aflame.

Dundee Pudding

2 tablespoons butter
3 tablespoons sugar
3 heaped tablespoons flour
3 tablespoons sponge cake crumbs
½ cup stoned raisins
2 apples
1½ teaspoons baking powder
2 tablespoons ground almonds
¼ teaspoon vanilla
2 eggs
Salt
Milk to mix

Beat sugar and butter to cream.

Mix crumbs, flour and baking powder together.

Beat flour and eggs alternately into butter and sugar.

Add chopped raisins, apples, ground almonds, salt and essence.

Mix all together, using a little milk if necessary.

Butter a mould, decorate with glacé cherries, pour in the mixture and steam for 2 hours.

Essex Pudding

3 tablespoons butter
4 tablespoons sugar
5 tablespoons flour
2 tablespoon strawberry jam
1 teaspoon bicarbonate of soda
2 eggs
Sufficient milk to mix

Beat the butter with the sugar to a cream.

Then add the eggs. These should be broken from the shells to the butter.

Beat after adding each egg.

Add flour and sufficient milk to make a smooth batter.

Mix in the strawberry jam and lastly the bicarbonate of soda.

Steam in buttered mould for 2 hours.

Fig Pudding

3 cups breadcrumbs
3 cups flour
1½ cups sugar
1½ cups suet (¾ lb)
¼ teaspoon bicarbonate of soda
2 cups figs cut into small pieces
1 egg
Butter milk or skim to mix

Mix the breadcrumbs with flour, sugar, finely chopped

suet, figs and bicarbonate of soda.

Mix all well together.

Beat an egg and stir it in, adding sufficient butter milk or skimmed milk to make a thick batter.

Pour into a buttered mould.

Cover with buttered paper and steam for 2½ hours.

Be careful that the batter is not too thin or figs will sink.

Jam and Marmalade Pudding

1 dessertspoon of marmalade
1 dessertspoon strawberry or raspberry jam
1 teaspoon bicarbonate of soda
1 egg
The weight of the egg in flour
The weight of the egg in breadcrumbs
½ the weight of the egg in butter

Break the egg and beat it well.

Melt the butter and add to the egg. Then beat in the flour and crumbs.

Dissolve the bicarbonate of soda in a little milk.

Add to the mixture together with the jam and marmalade.

Mix all very well. Put into a greased basin, which should not be more than ¾ full.

Tie down with greased paper and steam for 1½ hours.

Turn out carefully and serve with white sauce or custard sauce.

Vanilla Custard Sauce

2 egg yolks
2 tablespoons sugar
1 cup sugar
1 teaspoon vanilla essence

Beat the yolks and add sugar gradually.

Boil the milk and pour over the beaten egg yolks, beating all the time.

Thicken in double saucepan, stirring constantly.

Flavour with vanilla.

Jemima's Pudding

3 dessertspoons shortening
4 tablespoons sugar
2 eggs
2 cups flour
1 small teaspoon bicarbonate of soda, in enough warm water to dissolve
1 heaped tablespoon syrup
4 tablespoons fruit, currants or raisins
A little chopped candied peel
A little rum

Beat the eggs. Add the rum and bicarbonate of soda and mix with the other ingredients.

Have ready the pudding bowl in which a little syrup and butter have been nicely browned.

Steam for about 2 hours.

Steamed Macaroon Pudding

¼ cup butter
¼ cup sugar
3 eggs
½ lb stale white bread
¼ lb macaroons
1½ cups milk
Vanilla flavouring

Crumple and soak the bread and macaroons in the hot milk with the vanilla flavouring.

Add the sugar, butter and beaten egg yolks then add the stiffly beaten whites.

Butter a mould and then sprinkle with breadcrumbs.

Now put the mixture into the mould and steam for at least 1½ hours.

Serve hot at once with hot vanilla or fruit sauce.

Fruit sauce:

3 tablespoons jam, preferably apricot
½ cup water
2 tablespoons sugar

Boil until reduced to half and serve.

Melbourne Pudding

1½ cup flour
½ cup sugar
2 dessertspoons butter
2 dessertspoons jam
1 small teaspoon bicarbonate of soda
1 scant cup milk

Sift the flour. Add the sugar.

Rub in the butter and mix the jam in very well.

Add the milk slowly and beat the mixture thoroughly.

Mix the soda in a little milk, adding it to the mixture last and beat in well.

Steam for 2 hours. Serve with sauce.

Mincemeat Roly Poly

2 cups flour
1 cup suet
2 teaspoons baking powder
¼ teaspoon salt
Water to mix
Mincemeat

Sift together the flour, baking powder and salt.

Add the finely shredded suet.

Mix to a soft paste with the water.

Roll out until it is barely half an inch thick.

Spread it over evenly with mincemeat.

Roll it up in a floured cloth.

Tie the ends securely and boil steadily for 2 hours.

Mincemeat:

1 lb stoned raisins
¾ lb currants
6 ozs sultanas
¼ oz each of ground cloves, allspice, cinnamon and nutmeg
1 lb beef suet
1 lb of brown sugar
2 ozs chopped almonds
2 ozs each of chopped citron, lemon and orange peel

¼ oz salt
Rind and juice of 2 lemons
6 chopped apples
¼ pint of sherry
¼ pint of brandy

Mix all the ingredients well together and seal hermetically.

Novelty Pudding

1 small cup sugar
1 egg
1 tablespoon butter
2 large teaspoons baking powder
1 cup of milk
2 cups of flour
1 tablespoon cocoa
½ teaspoon ground cinnamon

Mix the butter and sugar to a cream.

Beat the egg well and mix with the milk.

Add to the sugar and butter.

Then add the flour.

Take half of the mixture and add the cocoa and cinnamon.

Mix together then put a spoonful of the two mixtures alternately into a buttered basin.

Cover with greased paper and steam for 2 ½ hours.

Serve with custard or cream.

Orange Pudding with Sauce

3 tablespoons sugar
1 teaspoon baking powder
1 egg
1 cup flour
1 cup suet
1 cup breadcrumbs
Grated rind and juice of 1 large orange
A little milk
A pinch of salt

Grate the rind of the orange and mix with the sugar.

Mix all dry ingredients together.

Strain and add the orange juice, the well beaten egg and sufficient milk to moisten the mixture.

Steam for at least 2 hours.

Sauce:

½ cup sugar
Grated rind and juice of 1 orange
1 dessertspoon cornflour (cornstarch)
1 cup water

Put the sugar, rind and juice of the orange in a small saucepan and bring to the boil.

Once boiling, add the cornflour previously mixed with a cup of water and cook for 10 minutes.

Peach Pudding

¼ cup butter
¾ cup flour
¼ cup semolina
3 tablespoons milk
1 egg
Sugar to taste
A small tin of peaches
A little almond essence
1 cherry for decoration

Drain the peaches well and dry them on a cloth. Grease a

basin.

Cut the peaches in halves and arrange them with the cherry in the centre, rounded side downwards and with the points to the centre (daisy pattern).

Sliced peaches may be used instead of whole ones.

Cream together the butter and sugar.

Beat the egg. Add it to the mixture and beat again.

Then add the semolina, sifted flour and a drop or two of almond essence together with the milk.

Put half of this mixture on to the peaches.

Then arrange the remaining fruit over this and lastly, cover with the rest of the mixture.

Cover with greased paper and steam for 1½ hours.

Use the juice from the peaches for a sauce.

Plain Suet Pudding

2 cups flour
1¼ cups finely chopped suet
1 teaspoon baking powder
A little water or milk for mixing
A pinch of salt

Mix dry ingredients well together with the suet.

Stir in as much cold water or milk to make a stiff paste.

Turn out onto a well floured cloth.

Tie the ends securely and plunge the pudding into fast boiling water.

Keep it boiling until done. It will take about 1½ hours.

Turn it upon a hot dish and serve with treacle, jam, marmalade.

Plum Pudding (Spotted Dick)

2 cups flour
1¼ cups finely chopped suet
1 teaspoon baking powder
A little water or milk for mixing
A pinch of salt
1 cup stoned raisins
1 cup of picked and dried currants
1 cup sugar
2 tablespoons candied peel, chopped small
1 egg
A little milk for mixing

Mix dry ingredients well together with the suet. Stir in as much cold water or milk to make a stiff paste.

Turn out onto a well floured cloth. Tie the ends securely and plunge the pudding into fast boiling water. Keep it boiling until done. It will take about 1½ hours.

Turn it upon a hot dish and serve with treacle, jam, marmalade.

Note:

If preferred, butter can be rubbed into the flour instead of suet and an additional teaspoonful of baking powder can be substituted for the egg.

Spiff Pudding

8 heaped tablespoons flour
6 tablespoons moist sugar
5 tablespoons butter
1 teaspoon bicarbonate of soda
1 heaped tablespoon cocoa
2 heaped tablespoons raisins
2½ cups milk

Pass the flour and cocoa through a sieve. Work in butter and sugar.

Heat the milk and add to the soda and mix at once to the dry ingredients.

Blend thoroughly.

Grease a mould and put the raisins in the bottom to form a cap.

Pour in the mixture and cover with greased paper.

Steam for 2 hours.

Sponge Pudding

2 tablespoons butter
2 tablespoons sugar
3 tablespoons milk
½ teaspoon baking powder
½ cup flour
1 egg

Cream the butter and sugar and work in the flour and egg alternately. Beat until smooth. Lastly, add the baking powder.

Put a little jam or marmalade at the bottom of a well greased basin and steam for 1½ hours.

Serve with white sauce.

White wine sauce:

3 egg yolks
1 egg white
3 tablespoons sugar
1½ cups white wine

Beat egg yolks and sugar together until smooth and light.

Bring wine to just below boiling point. Pour on egg mixture and let thicken a little over gentle heat. Do not allow to boil.

Beat the egg white until stiff. Fold into the sauce and serve.

Sweet Sauces

Brandy Sauce

1/3 cup butter
½ cup cream
1/2 cup powdered sugar
½ cup brandy
2 egg yolks

Cream the butter until light.

Add the sugar gradually then yolks of eggs.

Heat in double saucepan until it thickens, stirring all the time.

Add the cream and heat the brandy but do not boil.

Add to egg mixture and serve at once.

Brown Sugar Sauce

This recipe can be kept in a jar in the refrigerator and used at any time.

1 tablespoon butter
1 cup brown sugar
1 tablespoon flour
1 cup boiling water
1 teaspoon vanilla
1 egg

Melt butter.

Add flour and sugar.

Mix till smooth. Add boiling water.

Cook and stir until it is the consistency of molasses.

Pour this into egg that has been well beaten.

Do not cook after adding the egg.

Add flavouring.

Serve hot or cold on puddings or fruit cakes.

Caramel Sauce

1 cup sugar
½ cup cream

Put the sugar in a small saucepan and heat until a light brown, stirring continually.

Add the cream and cook until smooth.

Caramel Mocha Sauce

1 cup sugar
1 cup boiling water
¼ cup black coffee
1 teaspoon vanilla
A pinch of salt

Spread sugar on frying pan and heat until a light brown syrup is attained, (a few minutes only).

Add the boiling water very gradually and let simmer until all the sugar is dissolved.

Add the black coffee, salt and vanilla and cook until the desired thickness is obtained.

Fruit Sauce

3 tablespoons jam, preferably apricot
½ cup water
2 tablespoons sugar

Boil until reduced to half and serve.

Hot Chocolate Sauce

2 squares of chocolate
2 tablespoons butter
2 tablespoons syrup
1 teaspoon vanilla
½ cup boiling water
1 cup sugar
A pinch of salt

Melt the butter and chocolate and mix well.

Pour on the boiling water little by little.

Add the sugar and syrup and simmer for a few minutes.

Add the salt and vanilla.

Vanilla Custard Sauce

2 egg yolks
2 tablespoons sugar
1 cup sugar
1 teaspoon vanilla essence

Beat the yolks and add sugar gradually.

Boil the milk and pour over the beaten egg yolks, beating all the time.

Thicken in double saucepan, stirring constantly.

Flavour with vanilla.

Diplomatic Sauce

Yolks of 2 eggs
2 whole cloves
½ cup sugar
¼ cup of brandy
1 cup of red wine
A little lemon peel
A little salt

Heat but do not boil the wine.

Add brandy, lemon peel, cloves and salt.

Beat egg yolks until creamy with sugar, pour over the hot wine.

Thicken in a double saucepan, but do not allow to boil.

Strain.

Rummage Fruit Cream Sauce

¼ cup crystallized cherries
¼ cup crystallized figs or pineapples
¼ cup crystallized raisins
½ cup blanched almonds
1 cup sugar
1/2 cup cream
¼ cup brandy
¼ cup boiling water
A pinch of salt

Chop the fruit and nuts and soak in the brandy for 1 hour.

Boil together slowly the water, sugar and salt.

Add the cream and allow to boil for 1 minute.

Add nuts, fruit and brandy.

Serve hot or cold as the sweet requires.

White Wine Sauce

3 egg yolks
1 egg white
3 tablespoons sugar
1½ cups white wine

Beat egg yolks and sugar together until smooth and light.

Bring wine to just below boiling point.

Pour on egg mixture and let thicken a little over gentle heat.

Do not allow to boil.

Beat the egg white until stiff.

Fold into the sauce and serve.

Desserts with Gelatine

Gelatine

Gelatine is a product derived from collagen obtained from various animal by-products and used as a setting agent for sweet or savoury jellies and pudding fillings. It is translucent, tasteless, colourless and brittle when dry.

Household gelatine comes in the form of sheets or transparent leaves, granules, or powder. Instant types can be added to the food just as they are; others need to be soaked in water beforehand.

Sprinkle powdered gelatine over cold water and leave to soak and swell, then stir it into hot liquid until dissolved.

Soak leaf gelatine in a little cold liquid for a few minutes to soften, then squeeze out the excess moisture and add hot liquid to the leaves to dissolve them.

Vegetarians and vegans can substitute gelatine with agar-agar.

Tips:

- 2 ozs of gelatine will always set a quart of liquid.

- First rinse the mould in cold water and then pour in the jelly mixture.

- Also, stand the mould for 2 seconds in a bowl of hot water before turning out. In these ways there is less chance the jelly loses its shape.

Diana Baker

Babaroise

The recipe is sufficient for 4.

1 grated bar of chocolate
2 teaspoons of powdered gelatine
A little hot water
3 eggs
3 tablespoons fine sugar
A little vanilla essence

Grate up one bar of chocolate.

Melt it in a little hot water with ¼ teaspoon of gelatine and pour into mould.

Beat 3 egg whites quite stiff.

Add 3 tablespoons of fine sugar and the rest of the gelatine melted in a little hot water to the well whisked whites, a little vanilla essence and lastly the well beaten egg yolks.

Pour into mould on top of the chocolate and leave for 1 hour to set.

American Custard

4 teaspoons gelatine
3 cups milk
3 eggs
Nuts and cream to decorate
4 tablespoons fruit juice
1½ teaspoons almond or other extract
A pinch of salt

Heat the milk and salt in double boiler.

Add to this the gelatine dissolved in the fruit juice and stir well.

Beat the egg yolks and add to the hot milk mixture, cooking over hot water and stirring constantly until slightly thickened.

Remove from heat. Add flavouring.

Cool until slightly stiffened.

Beat egg whites. Add a little sugar to stiffen and fold into the custard.

Chill until set.

Decorate with whipped cream and chopped almonds or walnuts.

Apricot Custard Sponge

2 cups milk
½ cup sugar
3 eggs beaten lightly

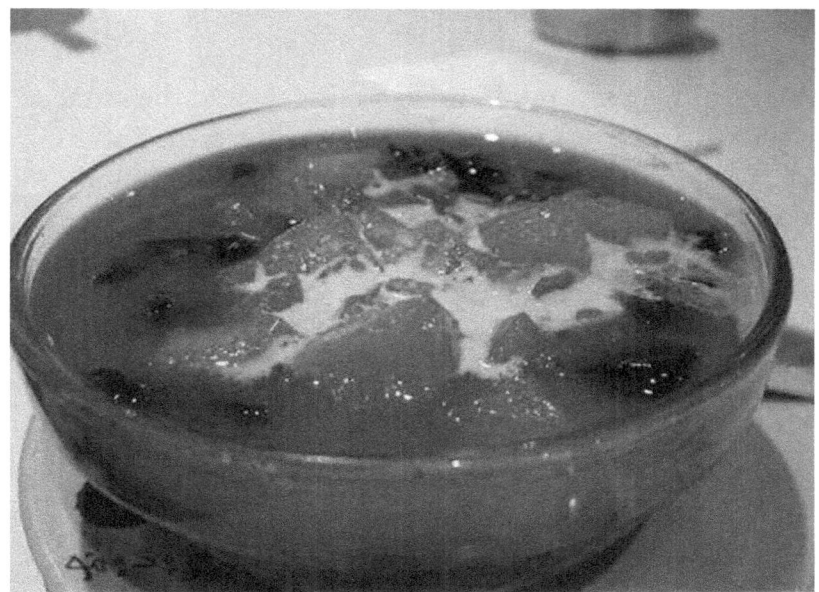

Make a boiled custard with the above three ingredients, cooking in a double boiler until mixture coats the spoon.

2 tablespoons gelatine
½ cup orange juice
1 tin of apricots
2 stiffly beaten egg whites
Sponge cake or lady fingers

Soak the gelatine in the orange juice.

Add to the custard the gelatine and orange juice. Add the apricot juice from the tin.

When cool, add the stiffly beaten egg whites.

Pour half the mixture into a wet mould, and place in refrigerator.

When almost set, put in the lady fingers and the crushed apricots and cover with the rest of the custard. Put in refrigerator till set. Turn out and serve with cream if desired.

Sherry Fluff

4 tablespoons boiling water
4 eggs
2 teaspoons powdered gelatine or 4 leaves of gelatine
4 tablespoons castor sugar

Beat the egg yolks with sugar.

Dissolve the gelatine in boiling water.

Add the yolks, beating well.

When nearly cold, add the flavouring of sherry.

Whip the whites of eggs to a stiff froth.

Mix together and pour into a dish to set.

Decorate with jam and whipped cream just before serving.

Diana Baker

Fruit and White Wine Jelly

3 cups water
1½ cups wine or champagne
¾ lb loaf sugar
1½ oz gelatine
2 egg whites

Fruit:

½ lb strawberries
½ cherries
Green glacé fruit cut lengthwise

Soak the fruit in a wine glass of rum or cherry brandy with the sugar.

To prepare the jelly:

Soak the gelatine and beat up the egg whites with a little cold water.

Put the water, sugar, egg whites and gelatine into a saucepan and stir with whisk until it boils and the gelatine is dissolved.

Strain through jelly bag.

Add the wine and allow to cool.

Pour a little into a wet border mould and put in refrigerator to set.

Now strain the fruit and put a little in mould.

Add more jelly and set again.

Then more fruit and finish by adding the remainder of the jelly.

When set turn out of mould and serve with the rest of the fruit in the centre.

Lemon Jelly

1 lemon
3 tablespoons sugar
1 cup water
1 oz gelatine
1 wineglass of sherry

Put the juice and rind of lemon into a pan with water, sugar and gelatine.

When warm add sherry and allow it to boil.

Strain into a wetted mould.

Alternate recipe:

6 lemons
1½ cups sugar
2 cups water
1½ oz gelatine

Dissolve the gelatine and sugar in the water over fire.

Squeeze the juice of the lemons into it.

Bring to the boil.

Strain through muslin and pour into a wetted mould.

Orange and Egg Jelly

4 eggs
1¼ cups sugar
4 oranges
2 lemons
4 teaspoons powdered gelatine

Beat the yolks together with sugar.

Mix the juice of oranges and lemons and add whites beaten to a stiff froth.

Pour in gelatine, which has been melted, beating very well all the time.

Beat for a short while then chill in the refrigerator until it sets.

Diana Baker

Plum Jelly

Plums
Powdered gelatine
Sugar to taste

Take some plums and cook with sugar to taste until soft.

Strain off liquid.

For every 2 cups of this liquid add 4 teaspoons powdered gelatine.

When dissolved strain into a mould and put in refrigerator.

Turn out and serve with cream.

Milk Gelatine

3 cups milk
2 or 3 tablespoons sugar
1½ measures of gelatine

Boil the milk with the sugar and flavouring.

Add the gelatine dissolved in a little milk or water.

Pour into a mould and cool to set.

Sunset Mousse

2 egg yolks
½ cup cold water
½ tablespoon instantaneous gelatine
1 cup golden syrup
1 dessertspoon lemon juice
1 cup whipped cream and extra for decorating

Boil up the syrup. Beat egg yolks in a bowl.

Stir in syrup very slowly.

Turn into saucepan and stir over heat till mixture thickens.

Remove from fire.

Add gelatine dissolved in the cold water.

Allow to stand till mixture begins to set.

Slightly stir in whipped cream and lemon juice.

Pour into a wet mould.

When required, serve turned out and decorated with whipped cream to taste.

Lemon Snow

This recipe is sufficient for 6 portions.

1 cup sugar
5 eggs
1 cup cream
Juice of 2 lemons
Rind of 1 lemon
3 teaspoons powdered gelatine

Put the gelatine to soak in cold water and leave for 5 minutes.

Beat the yolks well with the sugar until creamy and white.

Add the juice and rind of the lemons, the whites, previously beaten to a stiff froth, and lastly the gelatine.

Put into an unbreakable bowl over boiling water.

It is very important that the gelatine should be quite dissolved and warm.

Stir very slowly for a moment to avoid any gelatine remaining at the bottom of the bowl.

Serve in a glass dish decorated with whipped cream.

Snow Pudding

1 cup sugar
1 cup water
2 tablespoons gelatine
3 egg whites
1 teaspoon vanilla
¼ teaspoon almond extract

Boil sugar and water for 15 minutes.

Soak gelatine in a little cold water and then dissolve in the syrup.

Beat the whites very stiff and gradually add the syrup beating all the time. Continue beating for 20 minutes until very stiff.

Serve with whipped cream and nuts, or a soft custard sauce and shredded pineapple.

Vanilla custard:

2 egg yolks
2 tablespoons sugar
1 cup sugar
1 teaspoon vanilla essence

Beat the yolks and add sugar gradually.

Boil the milk and pour over the beaten egg yolks, beating all the time. Thicken in double saucepan, stirring constantly. Flavour with vanilla.

Cold Chocolate Soufflé

4 bars chocolate
2 cups milk
½ oz powdered gelatine
4 eggs
Vanilla and sugar to taste

Dissolve the chocolate in the milk.

Dissolve the gelatine in a little warm water.

Add the milk and chocolate.

Break the yolks into a glass dish and baet up with the sugar.

Add the milk, chocolate and gelatine and stir well.

When cool, fold in the stiffly beaten whites using two spoons until well mixed.

Place in refrigerator. Do not turn out.

Serve in same bowl.

Serve with whipped cream on top.

Spanish Cream

3½ cups milk
2 teaspoons powdered gelatine
2 eggs
2 tablespoons sugar
2 tablespoons strong coffee

Put the milk and gelatine in a pan and cook till the milk boils, when the gelatine will be dissolved.

Beat the yolks with the sugar in a large bowl.

Pour the hot milk over them, little by little, stirring constantly.

Return to the fire and stir till the mixture thickens over slow fire.

Remove before it boils and add flavouring.

Beat the whites of the eggs stiffly and add to the mixture.

Pour it into a wetted mould. Serve cold with cream.

Fruit Pies and Tarts

Pastry

- A cold temperature is necessary for the making of good pastry.

- A better result is obtained if the ingredients are put into the refrigerator for some time before needed.

- A little cream, milk or beaten egg brushed over the paste just before putting into the oven improves the colour.

Never-Fail Pie Crust for Beginners

This will make a 2 crust pie, or about a dozen tart shells.

2 cups flour
½ teaspoon salt
1 teaspoon baking powder
¾ shortening
1 egg yolk
2 tablespoons water, approximately depending on the flour used

Cream the shortening.

Add the flour, salt and sifted baking powder.

Cut into shortening with two knives until it is the size of peas.

Beat egg yolk and add water.

Add this egg and water mixture to flour and short mixture gradually until it holds together.

The less water in the pie crust the better.

Roll this on a floured board.

These can be baked on the reversed sides of muffin tins.

Bake for 12 minutes in hot oven.

Family Short Pastry

2 cups flour
¾ cup shortening
2 tablespoons sugar
2 teaspoons baking powder
2 tablespoons very hot water
A pinch of salt

Rub the fat into the flour and baking powder then stir in the sugar and salt.

Add the water and when all is mixed, knead well with your hands.

Bake about 20 minutes in a hot oven.

Rough Puff Pastry

1½ cups flour
4 to 6 tablespoons lard and butter mixed
A pinch of salt
A few drops of lemon juice
A little ice water for mixing
A little baking powder (optional)

Sift the flour and salt into a bowl.

Put in the fat and cut it up into pieces the size of a half walnut.

Mix the lemon juice with a very little water and add to the pastry, mixing with a knife to a firm dough.

Turn the pastry out on to a floured board.

Knead lightly to remove creases.

Roll out to an oblong strip about 14 inches long and 6 inches wide.

Make into three. Fold the bottom up to the middle and the top over it. Give it one half turn and roll out again. Repeat this three times.

Put it away to cool for as long as possible and use it for the same purposes as flaky pastry.

At first a very hot oven is required, reducing the heat towards the end of the cooking if necessary.

An Easy Piecrust to Try

Sponge fingers
5 tablespoons melted butter

Roll enough sponge fingers to make a cup of crumbs.

Mix thoroughly with the melted butter.

Line the bottom and sides of a 9" pie dish, pressing firmly into place.

Pour in filling as usual.

Scotch Apple Pie

4 cooking apples
1 clove or rind of lemon if preferred
Sugar to taste
6 tablespoons of flour
2 or 3 tablespoons of butter

Peel the apples and cut small.

Stew gently with sugar and the clove or rind of lemon.

Lay in a shallow dish or plate.

Put the flour in a bowl and rub in the butter until it crumbles.

Add 2 tablespoons of sugar.

Mix well with the fingers then drop the crumbs over the apples and bake in a quick oven for 10 to 15 minutes.

Tasty Apple Roll

1 lb short pastry
5 medium sized apples
1½ cups currants
½ cup sugar
1 teaspoon cinnamon
A little butter
1 egg yolk to brush

Core and slice the apples very thinly, and partially cook with sugar.

Roll the pastry fairly thin.

Spread with apples without the juice.

Sprinkle with the currants, sugar and cinnamon, adding a few dabs of butter.

Roll up in the form of a swiss roll being careful to seal ends with a little water.

Brush over with egg yolk.

Bake in a fairly hot oven.

Serve hot or cold.

Special Fruit Tart

This recipe can be used with fresh or tinned fruit of any kind to substitute for the apricots.

2 cups flour
2 teaspoons baking powder
1 cup butter
1 cup sugar
1 egg
1 tin apricots or stewed apricots cut in half
A pinch of salt

Mix the butter with the sugar. Add the egg, flour and other ingredients.

Place evenly on a round buttered and floured baking tin.

Bake in fairly slow oven. Remove from tin when cold and place the apricots over the paste, half of them with the cavity downwards and the other half with the cavity upwards.

Fill these with toasted and chopped almonds.

Reduce the syrup by mixing with a little apricot jam and turn it over the fruit.

Lastly, cover all with whipped cream.

Bakewell Tart

*½ lb short pastry
Strawberry jam
2 ozs butter
2 ozs castor sugar
2 ozs breadcrumbs
1 egg
A few ground almond
Almond flavouring
A little lemon juice*

Line a plate with the pasty and put a layer of jam in the centre, then a layer of ground almonds.

Cream the butter. Add sugar and beat in the egg.

Now add the breadcrumbs, flavouring and lemon juice. Mix well together.

Spread this filling also over the tart and bake in a moderately hot oven from 20 to 30 minutes.

Caramel Tart

2 tablespoons butter
1 cup brown sugar
1 tablespoon flour
2 egg yolks
1 cup milk
A little salt

Put the butter, sugar, flour and salt on the fire to melt.

Add the cup of milk.

Put in the yolks and cook in double saucepan until the mixture becomes as thick as lemon cheese.

Set aside to cool.

Line a plate with short crust. Prick well with a fork and bake in a quick oven.

Spread on the caramel mixture.

Beat the egg whites to a meringue.

Spread this on the caramel and put back in the oven to brown.

Citron Pudding or Tart

Puff pastry
3 egg yolks
½ pint of cream
1 tablespoon flour
2 ozs citron peel, cut thinly
Sugar to taste

Beat the yolks with the cream, the flour, citron peel and sugar.

Line a dish well with puff pastry and pour in the mixture.

Bake in a quick oven, then turn out and sprinkle with sugar.

Serve with wine sauce or sherry.

This can be served in cups without the pastry.

White Wine Sauce:

3 egg yolks
1 egg white
3 tablespoons sugar
1 ½ cups white wine

Beat egg yolks and sugar together until smooth and light.

Bring wine to just below boiling point.

Pour on egg mixture and let thicken a little over gentle

heat.

Do not allow to boil.

Beat the egg white until stiff.

Fold into the sauce and serve.

Coconut Pie

Short crust pastry
1 cup milk
½ cup coconut
2/3 cup sugar
2 eggs
A pinch of salt

Scald milk and pour while hot on to the coconut.

Beat eggs, sugar and salt together and add to milk and coconut.

Bake in a deep plate lined with short pastry.

Grape Tart

Pastry:
1½ cups flour
1 egg yolk
3 tablespoons sugar
4 ozs butter

Filling:
Crumbs of 4 sponge fingers
1½ lbs grapes
4 tablespoons sugar
3 tablespoons apricot jam

Proceed in the usual manner for all pastry.

Line in a special tart ring or mould, buttered and floured with the pastry.

Put in the crumbs, then fill with the peeled and seedless grapes, putting a few of the best ones aside for final decorating.

Dust with the sugar and bake in moderate oven for 20 to 30 minutes.

Remove from oven and when cold add the grapes left over.

Now strain the jam and boil up with equal quantities of water and sugar. Pour over the tart.

Note:
For a cold tart filling try stewed pears or stewed peaches in strawberry jelly and served with whipped cream.

Diana Baker

Easy Grape Tart

1 cup flour
2 teaspoons baking powder
1 dessertspoon sugar plus 2 tablespoons
1 tablespoon cold water
½ cup butter
A pinch of salt

Sift the flour, salt and baking powder together.

Add the sugar. Rub in the butter.

Put a piece of white paper, cut in half, on the table, placing one half slightly over the other.

Flour the paper and on this, gently roll out the paste.

Insert a knife under the pastry to loosen it from the paper.

Now raise it with the paper and place on baking plate, lightly buttered and floured, carefully removing the paper.

Wash and dry the grapes, selecting large ones.

Remove the seeds and fill the tart with them.

Dust over with 2 tablespoons of sugar.

Cook in moderate oven from 20 to 30 minutes.

Middle West Lemon Pie

Short crust pastry
¼ cup flour
1 cup boiling water
2 eggs
1 tablespoon butter
1 cup castor sugar
¼ teaspoon salt
Juice and grated rind of a lemon

Stir sugar, salt and flour together.

Add boiling water slowly. Then boil until clear, stirring constantly.

Add butter, slightly beaten egg yolks, lemon juice and rind.

When mixture is cool place in a baked pastry shell.

Beat whites of eggs stiffly.

Fold in 4 tablespoons of castor sugar and spread over the custard, sprinkle with castor sugar.

(This prevents the meringue becoming woolly).

Brown slightly in a very slow oven.

Mock Mince Pies

Short crust pastry
3 cooking apples
½ cup stoned raisins
½ cup sultanas
½ cup currants
1 tablespoon brown sugar
1 teaspoon mixed spice
1 tablespoon brandy
1 tablespoon melted butter
A pinch of salt

Peel the apples and cut very fine, then mix all the ingredients together.

Lay on a pie dish. Then place the pastry over the top and bake for about 30 minutes.

Orange Tart

This recipe is sufficient for 2 tarts and will keep good longer than ordinary pastry.

Pastry:

½ cup butter
½ cup sugar
2 cups butter
1 teaspoon cream of tartar
½ teaspoon bicarbonate of soda
1 egg

Filling:

1 cup sugar
1 cup water
1½ dessertspoons cornflour (cornstarch)
1½ dessertspoons custard powder
1 lemon
Juice of 1 large or 2 small oranges

Bring sugar and water to the boil.

Add the cornflour and custard powder mixed with the lemon and orange juice and cook for 5 minutes.

Cook the pastry, pricking well and when cool fill the pastry case with the filling.

When a little cooler, decorate with cream or meringue.

Orange Tartlets

Short crust pastry
½ cup sugar
2 egg yolks
2 tablespoons cake crumbs
1 orange, strained juice and grated rind
1 teaspoon lemon juice

Melt the butter in a saucepan.

Add the sugar and beaten egg yolks, then the juice and rind of the orange.

Stir well over low heat until mixture thickens (do not boil).

Stir in cake crumbs and lemon juice.

Put the mixture in tins lined with short pastry and bake in moderate oven for 30 minutes.

Raisin Nut Tart

Short crust pastry
1 cup chopped walnuts
2 cups seedless raisins
1¼ cups water
1 cup brown sugar
3 tablespoons cornflour
Grated rind and juice of 2 lemons
Grated rind and juice of 1 orange

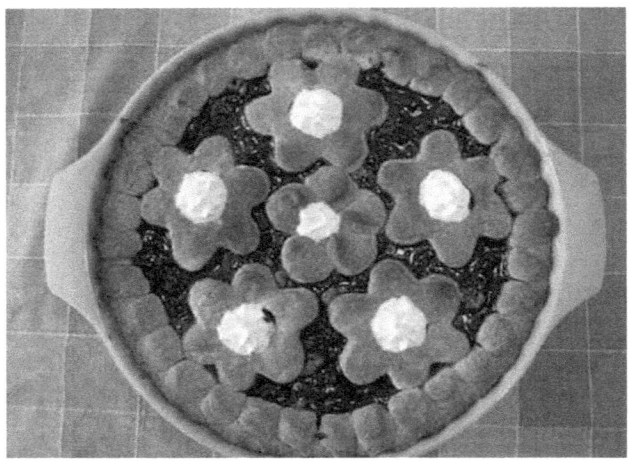

Line a deep sandwich tin with the pastry.

Cook together all the ingredients except the cornflour.

When the mixture boils, thicken it with the cornflour and water.

Put the mixture into the lined tin and cover with a lid of pastry strips.

Brush over with cold water and bake for 40 minutes.

When cold top with a little vanilla icing.

Rhubarb Tart

A pastry shell
1 cup sugar
1 egg
2 tablespoons flour
1½ lbs rhubarb
1 teaspoon lemon juice
The rind of ½ an orange, finely grated

Prepare the rhubarb and cut into 1 inch pieces.

Mix the sugar with the flour.

Add the well beaten egg, lemon juice and orange peel.

Beat all together.

Pour into an uncooked pastry shell, braid strips of pastry on the top.

Bake in a hot oven for 15 minutes, then reduce to moderate heat and cook 30 minutes more to cook the fruit.

Ice Cream

Carioca Ice Cream

2 cups sugar
4 cups water
2 cups shredded pineapple
2 egg whites
Juice of 1 lemon

Boil the water and sugar for 5 minutes.

Add the pineapple and allow to cool.

Add lemon juice and put into the freezer until set.

Remove mixture from tray and put into a cold basin and beat until light.

Add the stiffly beaten egg whites and return to tray and freeze.

Diana Baker

Burnt Ice Cream

1 tin peaches or large fruit
Ice cream
Vanilla
Burnt almonds
Cooking brandy

Drain the peaches well and place them in a rather flat silver dish.

Fill each peach with piled ice cream and stick in the almonds.

Heat the brandy and pour carefully into the dish.

Just before serving light the brandy and serve in flames.

Easy Ice Cream

1 small carton of cream
The same quantity of milk
½ teaspoon vanilla
½ cup icing sugar

Beat the cream until thick.

Add the milk and beat well.

Then add the icing sugar and continue to beat.

Now add the vanilla and continue beating.

Chill for 15 minutes.

Stir the mixture once again and then place into tray and freeze.

Lemon Cream

2 heaped tablespoons of cornflour (cornstarch)
1 pint of water
3 egg yolks
3 egg whites
1 cup sugar
Grated rind of 1 lemon

Dissolve the cornflour in the water and allow it to come to the boil.

Add the egg yolks, well beaten, the sugar and the grated rind of lemon.

Remove from the fire and add the well beaten whites.

Put into a mould and freeze.

Mocha Ice Cream

1 cup strong coffee
1 cup sugar
5 egg yolks
1½ cups cream
2 or 3 drops of vanilla essence

Beat the eggs with the sugar.

Add the coffee and thicken over a double boiler but do not allow to boil.

Leave to cool then beat over ice until frothy.

Add the slightly beaten cream and flavour with vanilla.

Put into mould and freeze.

Diana Baker

Fruity Ice Cream

2 cups mashed peaches
2 cups whipped cream
1 cup icing sugar
3 egg whites, stiffly beaten
1 tablespoon lemon juice

Sift the sugar.

Mix well with the fruit and lemon juice.

Fold in the whites and the cream.

Mix lightly.

Freeze in refrigerator tray.

Raspberry Ice Cream

The raspberries can be substituted for any easily mashed fruit.

2 cups raspberries
2 cups cream
1 cup sugar
2 egg whites
1 tablespoon lemon juice

Mix and mash the raspberries well with the sugar, until the sugar is quite dissolved, about 15 minutes.

Whip the cream adding 1 teaspoon sugar.

Add the stiffly beaten egg whites to the raspberries then lightly stir in the cream.

Freeze in refrigerator tray.

Russian Ice Cream

4 ozs chopped nuts
4 cups hot milk
1 cup sugar
6 egg yolks
½ cup cream
2 tablespoons crystallized fruits
1 wine glass liqueur

Boil together the milk and half the quantity of nuts for a few minutes.

Slightly beat up the yolks with the sugar.

Now strain the hot milk and stir gradually over the yolks.

Return to fire and stir until it thickens. Must not boil.

Allow to cool and add the cream, liqueur, nuts and finally the fruit.

Put into refrigerator tray and freeze.

Strawberry Ice Cream

1 cup mashed strawberries
1 cup cream,
Sugar to taste
Lemon juice

Add the pulp to the whipped cream.

Sweeten and flavour. Freeze.

Vanilla Ice Cream

2 ½ cups cream
5 egg yolks
2 teaspoons vanilla essence
¾ cup sugar
3 egg whites

Beat the yolks with the sugar for 10 minutes.

Whip the cream and add also the essence and the stiffly beaten whites.

Place in refrigerator tray and freeze.

Chocolate Ice Cream I

2½ cups cream
5 egg yolks
2 teaspoons vanilla essence
4 tablespoons grated chocolate dissolved in a very little water
¾ cup sugar
3 egg whites

Beat the yolks with the sugar for 10 minutes.

Whip the cream and add also the essence and the stiffly beaten whites.

Place in refrigerator tray and freeze.

Never-Fail Vanilla Ice Cream

This recipe is sufficient for 6 people.

The advantages of this recipe:

- There are only 3 ingredients
- Only 1 cup of cream
- Only stir once
- No cooking!

2/3 cup condensed milk
1½ teaspoons vanilla
1 cup whipping cream
½ cup water

Blend the condensed milk, water and essence thoroughly. Chill.

Whip the cream to a foamy, fluffy thickness only and fold into the chilled mixture.

Pour into a tray and freeze.

Remove from the freezer when the mixture is half frozen.

Scrape the mixture from the sides and bottom of the tray and beat until smooth but not melted.

Smooth out and replace in the tray until frozen and ready to serve.

Note:

1 tin of condensed milk makes 2 batches of ice cream.

Variations of Never-Fail Ice Cream

Coffee Ice Cream

2/3 cup condensed milk
½ teaspoon vanilla
1 cup whipping cream
1/2 cup strong black coffee

Blend the condensed milk, coffee and essence thoroughly. Chill.

Whip the cream to a foamy, fluffy thickness only and fold into the chilled mixture.

Pour into a tray and freeze.

Remove from the freezer when the mixture is half frozen.

Scrape the mixture from the sides and bottom of the tray and beat until smooth but not melted.

Smooth out and replace in the tray until frozen and ready to serve.

Orange Ice Cream

2/3 cup condensed milk
½ teaspoon grated orange rind
1 cup whipping cream
1/2 cup orange juice

Blend the condensed milk, orange juice and rind thoroughly. Chill.

Whip the cream to a foamy, fluffy thickness only and fold into the chilled mixture.

Pour into a tray and freeze.

Remove from the freezer when the mixture is half frozen.

Scrape the mixture from the sides and bottom of the tray and beat until smooth but not melted.

Smooth out and replace in the tray until frozen and ready to serve.

Tutti Frutti Ice Cream

2/3 cup condensed milk
1½ teaspoons vanilla
1 cup whipping cream
½ cup water
¼ cup finely chopped maraschino cherries
¼ cup seeded raisins, finely chopped

Blend the condensed milk, water and essence thoroughly. Chill.

Whip the cream to a foamy, fluffy thickness only and fold into the chilled mixture.

Pour into a tray and freeze.

Remove from the freezer when the mixture is half frozen.

Scrape the mixture from the sides and bottom of the tray and beat until smooth but not melted.

Now fold in the cherries and raisins.

Stir then replace in the tray and freeze until ready to serve.

Chocolate Ice Cream II

2/3 cup condensed milk
½ teaspoon vanilla
1 cup whipping cream
1 square of unsweetened melted chocolate

Blend the condensed milk, chocolate and essence thoroughly. Chill.

Whip the cream to a foamy, fluffy thickness only and fold into the chilled mixture.

Pour into a tray and freeze.

Remove from the freezer when the mixture is half frozen.

Scrape the mixture from the sides and bottom of the tray and beat until smooth but not melted.

Smooth out and replace in the tray.

Freeze until ready to serve.

Fresh Strawberry Ice Cream

2/3 cup condensed milk
1 cup whipping cream
½ cup water
1 cup crushed and sweetened strawberries
(approximately ¼ cup confectioner's sugar)

Blend the condensed milk and water. Chill.

Whip the cream to a foamy, fluffy thickness only and fold into the chilled mixture.

Add the strawberries and stir well. Pour into a tray and freeze.

Remove from the freezer when the mixture is half frozen.

Scrape the mixture from the sides and bottom of the tray and beat until smooth but not melted.

Smooth out and replace in the tray until frozen and ready to serve.

Diana Baker

Fresh Peach Ice Cream

2/3 cup condensed milk
1 cup whipping cream
½ cup water
1 cup crushed peaches

Blend the condensed milk and water thoroughly. Chill.

Whip the cream to a foamy, fluffy thickness only and fold into the chilled mixture.

Add the crushed peaches and stir well.

Pour into a tray and freeze.

Remove from the freezer when the mixture is half frozen.

Scrape the mixture from the sides and bottom of the tray and beat until smooth but not melted.

Smooth out and replace in the tray until frozen and ready to serve.

Dear Reader,

We are very interested in your comments and feedback on this work. Please help us by commenting on this book. You can do so by leaving a review after reading it in your e-book reader or at the store of purchase. You can also e-mail us at the following address: *info@editorialimagen.com*

For more books, visit the following site *Editorialimagen.com* to view new titles available and take advantage of the discounts and special prices we publish each week. You can contact us directly from there if you have any questions or suggestions. We look forward to hearing from you.

More Books

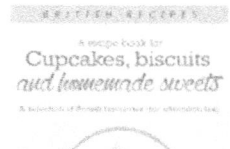

A Recipe Book for Cupcakes, Biscuits and Homemade Sweets – Selection of British Favourites.

Any time of day is the right time for something sweet or for a biscuit or cookie. In this recipe book for small cakes you'll find 114 recipes for delicious cupcakes, biscuits, scones, waffles, homemade bread, icings, fillings and homemade sweets.

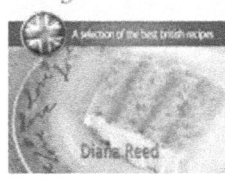

Cakes - English Favourites: A Selection of the Best British Recipes

More than 70 cake recipes for every occasion, from a simple sponge cake to a wedding cake, including fruit cakes, gingerbread, shortbread, pastries, chocolate cakes, icings, fillings, vinegar cakes and many more.

Spanish Related Books

Las Más Fáciles Recetas de Postres Caseros

Esta selección contiene recetas prácticas que, paso a paso, enseñan a preparar los postres, marcando el tiempo que se empleará, el coste económico, las raciones y los ingredientes.

Recetas Vegetarianas Fáciles y Baratas - Más de 100 recetas vegetarianas saludables y exquisitas

Si buscabas recetas de cocina vegetariana este libro de recetas veganas es para ti. El mismo es un recetario- que contiene una selección de recetas vegetarianas saludables y fáciles de preparar en poco tiempo. Este recetario incluye más de 100 recetas para toda ocasión, y contiene una serie de platos sin carnes ni pescados, con una variedad de recetas de Verduras, Huevos, Queso, Arroz, Ensaladas.

Recetario de Tortas con sabor inglés

Si buscabas recetas de cocina británica este libro es para ti. El mismo contiene una selección de recetas de tortas con sabor inglés. Este recetario incluye 80 recetas para toda ocasión, las cuales van desde lo más sencillo hasta lo más especial, como por ejemplo, una boda.

Recetas de Pescado y Salsas con sabor inglés

Recetas populares y a la vez muy fáciles, de la cocina británica. El recetario presenta diferentes maneras de cocinar el pescado, como así también tartas de pescado y salsas para acompañar el pescado.

Recetas de Sopas con sabor inglés

La sopa es un plato saturado de proteínas y nutrientes, es muy fácil de elaborar y además, apetece a cualquier hora del día. En la dieta inglesa la sopa es muy importante.

www.ingramcontent.com/pod-product-compliance
Lightning Source LLC
LaVergne TN
LVHW021715060526
838200LV00050B/2670